Kubernetes Handbook

A Non-Programmer's Guide

KUBERNETES
HANDBOOK

Non Programmer's Guide To Deploy
Applications With Kubernetes

STEPHEN FLEMING

5

Contents

BONUS TECHNOLOGY BOOKLET

Dear Friend,

I am privileged to have you onboard. You have shown faith in me and I would like to reciprocate it by offering the maximum value with an amazing booklet which contains latest technology updates on DevOps and Blockchain.

"Get Instant Access to Free Booklet and Future Updates"

- Link: http://eepurl.com/dge23r

OR

- QR Code : You can download a QR code reader app on your mobile and open the link:

Preface

This book has been well written as a guide to *getting started with Kubernetes, how they operate and how they are deployed*.

The book also explains the features and functions of Kubernetes and how it can be integrated into a total operational strategy for any project.

Additionally, the reader will be able to learn how to deploy real-world applications with Kubernetes.

The book has been written in a simple, easy to comprehend language and can be used by Non-Programmers, Project Managers, Business Consultants or any other persons with an interest in Kubernetes.

1. Introduction

Kubernetes Defined

Kubernetes, also known as K8s is an open-source container-orchestration system that can be used for programming deployment, scaling, and management of containerized applications. Kubernetes were innovated with the aim of providing a way of automatically deploying, scaling and running operations of container applications across a wide range of hosts. A container is a standalone, lightweight and executable package of a part of the software that is composed of components required to run it, i.e., system tools, code, runtime, system libraries, and settings. Containers function to segregate software from its adjacentenvironment, i.e., for instance, variances in development and staging environments thereby enabling the reduction of conflicts arising when teams run separate software on the same network infrastructure.

Containers may be flexible and really

9

fast, attributed to their lightweight feature, but they are prone to one problem: they have a short lifespan and are fragile. To overcome this enormous problem and increase the stability of the whole system, developers utilize Kubernetes to schedule and orchestrate container systems instead of constructing each small component, making up a container system bullet-proof. With Kubernetes, a container is easily altered and re-deployed when misbehaving or not functioning as required.

Kubernetes Background

The initial development of Kubernetes can be attributed to engineers working in industries facing analogous scaling problems. They started experimenting with smaller units of deployment utilizing cgroups and kernel namespaces to develop a process of individual deployment. With time, they developed containers which faced limitations, such that they were fragile, leading to a short lifetime; therefore, Google came up with an innovation calling it Kubernetes, a Greek name meaning "pilot" or "helmsman" in an effort aimed at sharing their own infrastructure and technology advantage with the community at large. The earliest founders were Joe Beda, Brendan Burns and Craig McLuckie who were later joined by Tim Hockin and Brian Grant from Google. In mid-2014, Google announced the development of Kubernetes based on its Borg System, unveiling a wheel with seven spokes as its logo which each wheel spoke representing a nod to the project's code name. Google released Kubernetes v1.0, the first version of their development on July 21, 2015, announcing that they had partnered with Linux Foundation to launch the Cloud Native Computing Foundation (CNCF) to promote further innovation and development of the Kubernetes. Currently, Kubernetes provides organizations with a way of effectively dealing with some of the main management and operational concerns faced in almost all organizations worldwide, by offering a solution for

11

administration and managing several containers deployed at scale, eliminating the practice of just working with Docker on a manually-configured host.

Advantages Of KUBERNETES

While Kubernetes was innovated to offer an efficient way of working with containers on Google systems, it has a wider range of functionalities and can be used essentially by anyone regardless of whether they are using the Google Compute Engine on Android devices. They offer a wide range of advantages, with one of them being the combination of various tools for container deployments, such as orchestration, services discovery and load balancing. Kubernetes promotes interaction between developers, providing a platform for an exchange of ideas for the development of better versions. Additionally, Kubernetes enables the easy discovery of bugs in containers due to its beta version.

2. How Kubernetes Operates

Kubernetes design features a set of components referred to as primitives which jointly function to provide a mechanism of deploying, maintaining and scaling applications. The components are loosely coupled with the ability to be extensible to meet a variety of workloads. Extensibility is attributed to the Kubernetes API, which is utilized by internal components coupled with extensions and containers that operates on Kubernetes. In simple, understandable terms, Kubernetes is basically an object store interacting with various codes. Each object has three main components: the metadata, a specification and a current status that can be observed; therefore, a user is required to provide metadata with a specification describing the anticipated state of the objects. Kubernetes will then function to implement the request by reporting on the progress under the status key of the object.

The Kubernetes architecture is composed of various pieces which work together as an interconnected package. Each component at play has a specified role, some of which are discussed below. Additionally, some components are placed in the container/cloud space.

- **Master**- It is the overall managing component which runs one or more minions.

- **Minion** –Operates under the master to accomplish the delegated task.

- **Pod**- A piece of application responsible for running a minion. It is also the basic unit of manipulation in Kubernetes.

- **Replications Controller**- *Tasked with confirming that the requested number of pods are* running on minions every time.

- **_Label_**- Refers to a key used by the Replication Controller for service discovery.

- **_Kubecfg_**- A command line used to configure tools.

- **_Service_**- Denotes an endpoint providing load balancing across a replicated group of pods.

With these components, Kubernetes operate by generating a master which discloses the Kubernetes API, in turn, allowing a user to request the accomplishment of a certain task. The master then issues containers to perform the requested task. Apart from running a Docker, each node is responsible for running the Kubelet service whose main function is to operate the container manifest and proxy service. Each of the components is discussed in detail in this chapter.

Docker and Kubernetes

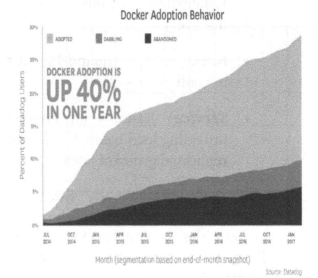

Source: Datadog

While Docker and Kubernetes may appear similar and help users run applications within containers, they are very different and operate at different layers of the stack, and can even be used together. A Docker is an open source package of tools that help you "Build, Ship, and Run" any app anywhere, and also enables you to develop and create software with containers. The use of a Docker involves the creation of a particular file known as a Dockerfile

16

which defines a build process and produces a Docker image when the build process is integrated to the 'Docker build' command. Additionally, Docker offers a cloud-based repository known as the Docker Hub which can be used to store and allocate the created container images. Think of it like GitHub for Docker Images. One limitation involved in the use of Docker is that a lot of work is involved in running multiple containers across multiple devices when using microservices. For instance, the process involves running the right containers at the right time; therefore, you have to work out how the containers will communicate with each other, figure out storage deliberations and handle or redeploy failed containers or hardware. All this work could be a nightmare, especially when you are doing it manually; therefore, the need for Kubernetes.

Unlike Docker, Kubernetes is an open-source container orchestration platform which allows lots of containers to harmoniously function together automatically, rather than integrating every container separately across multiple machines, thus cutting down the operational cost involved. Kubernetes has a wide range of functions, some of which are outlined below:

- Integrating containers across different machines.

- Redeploying containers on different machines in case of system failure.

- Scaling up or down based on demand changes by adding or removing containers.

- They are essential in maintaining the consistent storage of multiple instances of an application.

- Important for distributing load between containers.

As much as Kubernetes is known for container management, Docker also can manage containers using its own native container management tool known as Docker Swarm, which enables you to independently deploy containers as Swarms which then interact as a single unit. It is worth noting that Kubernetes interacts only with the Docker engine itself and never with Docker Swarm.

As mentioned above, Kubernetes can be integrated with the Docker engine with an intention of co-coordinating the development and execution of Docker containers on Kubelet. In this type of integration, the Docker engine is tasked with running the actual container image built by running 'Docker build.' Kubernetes, additionally, handles higher level concepts, including service-discovery, load balancing, and network policies.

Interestingly, as much as Docker and Kubernetes are essentially different from their core, they can be used concurrently to efficiently develop modern cloud architecture by facilitating the management and deployment of containers in the distributed architecture.

Containers are the new packaging format because they're efficient and portable

- App Engine supports Docker containers as a custom runtime
- Google Container Registry: private container image hosting on GCS with various CI/CD integrations

- Compute Engine supports containers, including managed instance groups with Docker containers
- The most powerful choice is a container **orchestrator**

Pods: Running Containers in Kubernetes

Pods area group of containers and volumes which share the same resource - usually an IP address or a file system, therefore allowing them to be scheduled together. Basically, a pod denotes one or more containers that can be controlled as a single application. A pod can be described as the most basic unit of an application that can be used directly with Kubernetes and consists of containers that function in close association by sharing a lifecycle and should always be scheduled on the same node. Coupled containers condensed in a pod are managed completely as a single unit and share various components such as the environment, volumes and IP space.

Generally, pods are made into two classes of containers: a main container which functions to achieve the specified purpose of the workload and some helper containers which can optionally be used to accomplish closely-related tasks. Pods are tightly tied to the main application, however, some applications may benefit by being run and managed in their containers. For instance, a pod may consist of one container running the primary application server and a helper container extracting files to the shared file system, making an external repository detect the changes. Therefore, on the pod level, horizontal scaling is generally discouraged as there are other higher level tolls best suited for the task.

It is important to note that Kubernetes schedules and orchestrates functionalities at the pod level rather than the container level; therefore, containers running in the same pod have to be managed together in a concept known as the shared fate which is key in the underpinning of any clustering system. Also, note that pods lack durability since the master scheduler may expel a pod from its host by deleting the pod and creating a new copy or bringing in a new node.

Kubernetes assigns pods a shared IP enabling them to communicate with each other through a component called a localhost address, contrary to Docker configuration where each pod is assigned a specific IP address.

Users are advised against managing pods by themselves as they do not offer some key features needed in an application, such as advanced lifecycle management and scaling. Users are instead invigorated to work with advanced level objects which use pods or work with pod templates as base components to implement additional functionality.

Replication and Other Controllers

Before we discuss replication controllers and other controllers, it is important to understand Kubernetes replication and its uses. To begin with, being a container management tool, Kubernetes was intended to orchestrate multiple containers and replication. Replication refers to creating multiple versions of an application or container for various reasons, including enhancing reliability, load balancing, and scaling. Replication is necessary for various situations, such as in microservices-based applications to provide specific functionality, to implement native cloud applications and to develop mobile applications. Replication controllers, replica sets, and deployments are the forms of replications and are discussed below:

Replication Controller

A replication controller is an object that describes a pod template and regulates controls to outline identical replicas of a pod horizontally by increasing or decreasing the number of running copies. A Replication controller provides an easier way of distributing load across the containers and increasing availability natively within Kubernetes. This controller knows how to develop new pods using a pod template that closely takes after a pod definition which is rooted in the replication controller configuration.

The replication controller is tasked to ensure that the number of pods deployed in a cluster equals the number of pods in its configuration. Thus, in case of failure in a pod or an underlying host, the controller will create new pods to replace the failed pods. Additionally, a change in the number of replicas in the controller's configuration, the controller will either initiate or kill containers to match the anticipated number. Replication controllers are also tasked to carry out rolling updates to roll over a package of pods to develop a new version, thus minimizing the impact felt due to application unavailability.

Replication Sets

Replication sets are an advancement of replication controller design with greater flexibility with how the controller establishes the pods requiring management. Replication sets have a greater enhanced replica selection capability; however, they cannot perform rolling updates in addition to cycling backends to a new version. Therefore, replication sets can be used instead of higher level units which provide similar functionalities.

Just like pods, replication controllers and replication sets cannot be worked on directly as they lack some of the fine-grained lifecycle management only found in more complex tools.

Deployments

Deployments are meant to replace replication controls and are built with replication sets as the building blocks. Deployments offer a solution to problems associated with the implementation of rolling updates. Deployments are advanced tools designed to simplify the lifecycle of replicated pods. It is easy to modify replication by changing the configuration which will automatically adjust the replica sets, manage transitions between different versions of the same application, and optionally store records of events and reverse capabilities automatically. With these great features, it is certain that deployment will be the most common type of replication tool used in Kubernetes.

Master and Nodes

Initially, minions were called nodes, but their names have since been changed back to minions. In a collection of networked machines common in data centers, one machine hosts the working machines. The working machines are known as nodes. The master machine is responsible for running special co-ordinating software that schedules containers on the nodes. A collection of masters and nodes are known as clusters. Masters and nodes are defined by the software component they run. The master is tasked to run three main items:

- API Server - The API server ensures that all the components on the master and nodes achieve their respective tasks by making API calls.

- Etcd - This is a service responsible for keeping and replicating the current configuration and run the state of the cluster. It is implemented as a lightweight distributed key-value store.

- Scheduler and Controller Manager- These processes schedule containers, specifically pods, onto target nodes. Additionally, they may correct numbers of the running processes.

A node usually carries out three important processes, which are discussed below:

- Kubelet- It is an advanced background process (daemon) that runs on each node and functions to respond to commands from the master to create, destroy and monitor containers on that host.

- Proxy - It is a simple network proxy that can be used to separate the IP address of a target container from the name of the services it provides.

- cAdvisor- It is an optional special daemon that collects, aggregates, processes, and exports information about running containers. The information may exclude information on resource isolation, historical usage, and key network statistics.

The main difference between a master and a node is based on the set of the process being undertaken.

The 10,000-foot view

users   master   nodes

Services

A service assigns a fixed IP to your pod replicas and allows other pods or services to communicate with them

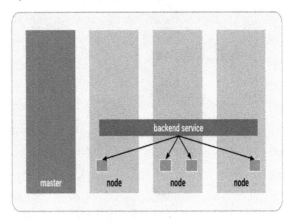

In Kubernetes, a service is an important component that acts a central internal load balancer and representatives of the pods. Services can also be defined as a long-lasting, well-known endpoint that points to a set of pods in a cluster. Services consist of three critical components: an external IP address (known as a portal, or sometimes a portal IP), a port and a label selector. Service is usually revealed through a small proxy process. The service proxy is responsible for deciding which pod to route to an endpoint request via a label selector. It also acts as a thin look-up service to determine a way of handling the request. The service proxy is, therefore, in simple terms, a tuple that maps a portal, port, and label selector.

A service abstraction is essential to allow you to scale out or replace the backend work units as necessary. A service's IP address remains unchanged and stable regardless of the changes to the pods it routes too. When you deploy a service, you are simply gaining discoverability and can simplify your container designs. A service should be configured any time you need to provide access to one or more pods to another application or external consumers. For example, if you have a set of pods running web servers that should be accessible from the internet, a service will provide the necessary concept. Similarly, if a web service needs to store and recover data, an internal service is required to authorize access to the database pods.

In most circumstances, services are only

available via the use of an internally routable IP address. However, they can also be made available from their usual places through the use of several strategies, such as the NodePort configuration which works by opening a static port on each node's external networking interface. In this strategy, the traffic to the external port is routed automatically using an internal cluster IP service to the appropriate pods. Instead, the Load Balancer service strategy can be used to create an external load balancer which, in turn, routes to the services using a cloud provider's load balancer integration. The cloud controller manager, in turn, creates an appropriate resource and configures it using an internal service address. In summary, the main functionality of services in Kubernetes is to expose a pod's unique IP address which is usually not exposed outside the cluster without a service.

You can have multiple services with different configurations and features

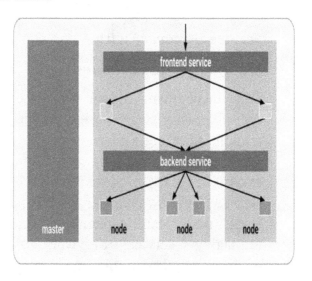

Service Discovery

Service discovery refers to the process of establishing how to connect to a service. Services need dynamically to discover each other to obtain IP addresses and port detail which are essential in communicating with other services in the cluster. Kubernetes offers two mechanisms of service discovery: DNS and environmental variable. While there is a service discovery option based on environmental variables available, most users prefer the DNS-based service discovery. Both are discussed below.

Service Discovery with

Environmental Variables

This mechanism of service discovery occurs when a pod exposes a service on a node, initiating Kubernetes to develop a set of environmental variables on the exposed node to describe the new service. This way, other pods on the same node can consume it easily. Managing service discovery using environmental variable mechanism is not scalable, therefore, most people prefer the Cluster DNS to discover services.

Cluster DNS

Cluster DNS enables a pod to discover services in the cluster, thereby enabling services to communicate with each other without having to worry about IP addresses and other fragile schemes. With cluster DNS, you can configure your cluster to schedule a pod and service that expose DNS. Then, when new pods are developed, they are informed of this service and will use it for look-ups. The cluster DNS is made of three special containers listed below:

- Etcd - Important for storing all the actual look-up information.

- SkyDns- It is a special DNS server written to read from etcd.

- Kube2sky - It is a Kubernetes-specific program that watches the master for any changes to the list of services and then publishes the information into etcd. SkyDns will then pick it up.

Apart from environmental variables and cluster DNS, there are other mechanisms which you can use to expose some of the services in your cluster to the rest of the world. This mechanism includes Direct Access, DIY Load Balancing, and Managed Hosting.

Direct Access- Involves configuring the firewall to pass traffic from the outside world to the portal IP of your service. Then, the proxy located on the node selects the container requested by the service. However, direct access faces a problem of limitation where you are constrained to only one pod to service the request, therefore, fault intolerant.

DIY Load Balancing- Involves placing the load balancer in front of the cluster and then populating it with the portal IPs of your service; therefore, you will have multiple pods available for the service request.

Managed Hosting- Most cloud providers supporting Kubernetes offer an easier way to make your services discoverable. All you need to do is to define your service by including a flag named *CreateExternalLoadBalncer* and set its value to *true*. By doing this, the cloud provider automatically adds the portal IPs for your service to a fleet of load balancers that is created on your behalf.

ReplicaSets-Replica Set Theory/Hands-on with ReplicaSets

As mentioned earlier, ReplicaSets is an advanced version of Replication Controller, offering greater flexibility in how the controller establishes the pods it is meant to manage. A ReplicaSet ensures that a specified number of pod replicas are running at any given time. Deployment can be used to effectively manage ReplicaSets as it enables it to provide declarative updates to pods combined with a lot of other useful features.

Using ReplicaSets is quite easy since most Kubernetes commands supporting Replication Controllers also support ReplicaSets except the rolling update command which is best used in Deployments. While ReplicaSets can be used independent of each other, it is best used by Deployments as a mechanism of orchestrating pod creation, deletion, and updates. By using

Deployments, you will not have to worry about managing the ReplicaSets they develop as they deploy and manage their ReplicaSets.

Daemon Sets

Daemon Sets are a specialized form of pod controller which runs a copy of a pod on each node in the cluster (or a subset, if specified). Daemon Sets are useful when deploying pods which help perform maintenance and provide services for the nodes themselves by creating pods on each added node, and garbage collects pods when nodes are removed from the cluster. Daemon Sets can be used for running daemons that require running on all nodes of a cluster. Such things can be cluster storage daemons, such as Qubyte, ceph, glusterd, etc., log collectors such as Fluentd or Logstash, or monitoring daemons such as Prometheus Node Exporter, Collectd, New Relic agent, etc.

The daemon can be deployed to all nodes, but it's important to split a single daemon to multiple daemons. Note that in situations involving a cluster with nodes of different hardware requiring adaption in the memory and CPU, you may have to include for the daemon for effective functionality.

There are other cases where you may require different logging, monitoring, or storage solutions on separate nodes of your cluster. In such circumstances where you prefer to deploy the daemons only to a specific set of nodes rather than the entire node, you may use a node selector to specify a subdivision of the nodes linked to the Daemon Set. For this to function effectively, you should have labeled your nodes consequently.

There are four main mechanisms in which you can communicate to the daemons discussed below:

- Push - In this mechanism, the pods are configured to push data to a service, making the services undiscoverable to clients.

- NodeIP and known port - The pods utilize a host port, enabling clients to access each NodeIP via this port.

- DNS - In this mechanism, pods are accessed via a headless service by either the use of an endpoints resource or obtaining several A Records from DNS.

- Service - The pods are accessible via the standard service. The client can access a daemon on a random node using the same service; however, in this mechanism, you may not be able to access a specific node.

Since Daemon Sets are tasked to provide essential services and are required throughout the fleet, they, therefore, are allowed to bypass pod scheduling restrictions which limit other controllers from delegating pods to certain hosts. For instance, attributed to its unique responsibilities, the master server is usually configured to be inaccessible for normal pod scheduling, providing Daemon Sets with the ability to override the limitation on the pod-by-pod basis to ensure that essential services are running.

As per now, Kubernetes does not offer a mechanism of automatically updating a node. Therefore, you can only use the semi-automatic way of updating the pods by deleting the daemon set with the –cascade=false option, so that the pods may allot on the nodes; then you can develop a new Daemon Set with an identical pod selector and an updated pod template. The new Daemon Set will automatically recognize the previous pods, but will not automatically update them; however, you will need to use the new pod templates after manually deleting the previous pods from the nodes.

Jobs

Jobs are workloads used by Kubernetes to offer a more task-built workflow where the running containers are expected to exit successfully after completing the workload. Unlike the characteristic pod which is used to run long-running processes, jobs allow you to manage pods that are required to be terminated rather than being redeployed. A job can create one or more pods and guarantees the termination of a particular number of pods. Jobs can be used to achieve a typical batch-job such as backing up a database or deploying workers that need to function off a specific queue, i.e., image or video converters. There are various types of jobs as discussed below:

Non-parallel Jobs

In this type of job, one pod is usually initiated and goes on to complete the job after it has been terminated successfully. Incase of a failure in the pod, another one is created almost immediately to take its place.

Parallel Job with a fixed completion count

In a parallel job with a fixed completion count, a job is considered complete when there is one successful pod for every value between 1 and the number of completions specified.

Parallel Jobs with a work queue

With parallel jobs with a work queue, no pod is terminated lest the work queue is empty. This means that even if the worker performed its job, the pod could only be terminated successfully when the worker approves that all its fellow workers are also done. Consequently, all other pods are required to be terminated in the process of existing. Requested parallelism can be defined by parallel Jobs. For instance, if a job is set to 0, then the job is fundamentally paused until it is increased. It is worth noting that parallel jobs cannot support situations which require closely-communicating parallel processes, for example, in scientific computations.

CronJobs

CronJobs are used to schedule jobs or program the repetition of jobs at a specific point in time. They are analogous to jobs but with the addition of a schedule in Cron format.

ConfigMaps and Secrets

Kubernetes offers two separate storage locations for storing configuration information: Secrets for storing sensitive information and ConfigMaps for storing general configuration. Secrets and ConfigMaps are very similar in usage and support some use cases. ConfigMaps provides a mechanism of storing configuration in the environment rather than using code. It is important to store an application's configuration in the environment since an application can change configuration through development, staging, production, etc.; therefore, storing configuration in the environment increases portability of applications. ConfigMaps and Secrets are discussed below in detail.

Secrets

As mentioned above, Secrets are important for storing miniature amounts, i.e., less than I MB each of sensitive information such as keys, tokens, and passwords, etc. Kubernetes has a mechanism of creating and using Secrets automatically, for instance, Service Account token for accessing the API from a pod and it is also easy for users to create their passwords. It is quite simple to use passwords; you just have to reference them in a pod and then utilize them as either file at your own specified mount points, or as environmental variables in your pod. Note that each container in your pod is supposed to access the Secret needs to request it explicitly. However, there is no understood mechanism of sharing of Secrets inside the pod.

PullSecrets are a special type of Secret that can be used to bypass a Docker or another container image registry login to the Kubelet so that it can extract a private image for your pod. You need to be extremely cautious when updating Secrets that are in use by running pods since the pods in operation would not automatically pull the updated Secret. Additionally, you will need to explicitly update your pods, i.e., using the rolling update functionality of Deployments discussed above, or by restarting or recreating them. Put in mind that a Secret is namespaced, meaning that they are placed on a specific namespace, and only pods in the same namespace can access the Secret.

Secrets are stored in tmpfs and only stored on nodes that run pods which utilize those Secrets. The tmpfs keep Secrets from being accessible by the rest of the nodes in an application. Secrets are transmitted to and from the API server in plain text; therefore, you have to implement the SSL/TLS protected connections between user and API server and additionally between the API server and kubelets.

To enhance security for secrets, you should encrypt secrets in etcd. To add another layer of security, you should enable Node Authorization in Kubernetes, so that a kubelet can only request Secrets of Pods about its node. This function is to decrease the blast radius of a security breach on a node.

ConfigMaps

ConfigMaps are arguably similar to Secrets, only that they are designed to efficiently support working with strings that do not contain sensitive information. ConfigMaps can be used to store individual properties in the form of key-value pairs; however, the values can also be entirely used to configure files or JSON blobs to store more information. Configuration data can then be used to:

- Configure the environmental variable.

- Command-line arguments for a container.

- Configure files in a volume.

- Storing configuration files for tools like Redis or Prometheus which allows you to change the configuration of containers without having to rebuild the entire container.

ConfigMaps differs from Secrets in that it necessarily gets updated without the need to restart the pods which use them. Nevertheless, depending on how to implement the configuration provided, you may need to reload the configs, e.g., using an API call to Prometheus to reload. This is often done through a sidecar container in the same pod watching for changes in the config file.

The most important thing about ConfigMaps and Secrets is that they function to enhance the versatility of containers by limiting their specificities which allow users to deploy them in different ways. Therefore, users are provided with a choice of reusing containers or among teams, or even outside the organization due to the elimination of container specificity. Secrets are especially helpful when sharing with other teams and organizations, or even when sharing publicly. This enables you to freely share images, for instance, via a public respiratory, without having to worry about any company-specific or sensitive data being published.

How is it going till now? Before moving to the deployment part just recap the topics you just went through. Also, can you spare some time and review the book?

3. Deployments

In Kubernetes, deployments are essential for deploying and managing software; therefore, it is important to comprehend how they function and how to use effectively. Before deployment, there were Replication Controllers, which managed pods and ensured a certain number of them were operating. With deployments, we moved to ReplicaSets, which replaced Replication Controllers later on. ReplicaSets are not usually managed; rather they get managed by Deployments we define through a definite chain, i.e., Deployment-ReplicaSet-Pod(s). In addition to what ReplicaSets offer, Deployment offers you declarative control over the update strategy used for the pods. This replaces the old kubectl rolling-update way of updating, but offers similar flexibility regarding defining maxSurge and maxUnavailable,

50

i.e., how many additional and how many unavailable pods are allowed.

Deployments can manage your updates and even go as far as checking whether or not a new version being rolled out is working, and stop the rollout in case it is not. Additionally, you can indicate a wait time needed by a pod to be ready without any of its containers crashing before it's considered available, prevents "bad updates" giving your containers plenty of time to get ready to handle traffic. Furthermore, Deployments store a history of their revisions which can be used in rollback situations, as well as an event log, that can be used to audit releases and changes to your Deployment.

Integrating Storage Solutions and Kubernetes

Today, organizations are struggling to deliver solutions which will allow them to meet quickly changing business needs, as well as to address competitive pressure. To achieve this, they are utilizing various technologies such as containers, Kubernetes, and programmable infrastructure to achieve continuous integration/continuous development (CI/CD) and DevOps transformations.

For organizations deploying these technologies, they have to ensure tenacious storage across containers as it is important to maximize the number of applications in the model. One such example of an integrated storage solution which can be integrated to Kubernetes is NetApp Trident which is discussed in detail below.

NetApp Trident

Unlike competitive application container orchestration and dynamic storage provisioning plugins, NetApp Trident integrates with Kubernetes' persistent volume (PV) framework. Red Hat OpenShift with Trident provides one interface for dynamic provision of a persistent volume of applications across storage classes. These interfaces can be allocated to any of the storage platforms from NetApp to deliver the optimal storage management capabilities and performance for each application.

Trident was developed as an open source project by NetApp to offer Kubernetes users an external mechanism of monitoring Kubernetes volume and to completely automate the provisioning process. Trident can be integrated to Kubernetes and deployed as a physical server for storage, a virtual host, or a Kubernetes Pod. Trident offers Kubernetes a persistent storage solution and can be used in situations such as:

- In cloud-native applications and microservices.

- Traditional enterprise applications deployed in a hybrid cloud.

- DevOps teams who want to accelerate the CI/CD pipeline.

Trident also provides a boost of advanced features which are designed to offer deployment flexibility in

Kubernetes containerized applications, in addition to providing basic persistent volume integration. With Trident, you can:

- Configure storage via a simple Representational State Transfer application programming interface (REST API) with unique concepts that contain specific capabilities to Kubernetes storage classes.

- Protect and manage application data with NetApp enterprise-class storage. Current storage objects, such as volumes and logical unit numbers (LUNs), can easily be used by Trident.

- Based on your choice, you can use separate NetApp storage backends and deploy each with different configurations, thus allowing Trident to provide and consume storage with separate features, and present that storage to container-deployed workloads in a straightforward fashion.

Integrating the Trident dynamic storage provider to Kubernetes as a storage solution offers numerous benefits outlined below:

- Enables you to develop and deploy applications faster with rapid iterative testing.

- It provides a dynamic storage solution across storage classes of the entire storage portfolio of SolidFire, E-Series, NetApp, and ONTAP storage platforms.

- Improves efficiency when developing applications using Kubernetes.

Deploying Real World Application

To give you a better idea on how to deploy the real-world application, we are going to use a real-world application, i.e., Parse.

Parse

Parse is a cloud API designed to provide easy-to-use storage for mobile applications. It offers a variety of different client libraries making it easy to integrate with Android, iOS and other mobile platforms. Here is how you can deploy Parse in Kubernetes:

Fundamentals

Parse utilizes MongoDB cluster for its storage, therefore, you have to set up a replicated MongoDB using Kubernetes StatefulSets. Additionally, you should have a Kubernetes cluster deployed and ensure that the kubectl tool is properly configured.

Building the parse-server

The open source parse-server comes with a Dockerfile for easy containerization of the clone Parse repository.

```
$ git clone
https://github.com/ParsePlatform/pars
e-server
```

Then move into that directory and build the image:

$ cd parse-server

$ docker build -t ${DOCKER_USER}/parse-server.

Finally, push that image up to the Docker hub:

$ docker push ${DOCKER_USER}/parse-server

Deploying the parse-server

Once a container image is developed, it is easy to deploy the parse-server into your cluster using the environmental variables configuration below:

APPLICATION-ID-An identifier for authorizing your application.

MASTER-KEY-An identifier that authorizes the master user.

DATABASE-URI-It is the URI for your MongoDB cluster.

When all these are placed together, it is

possible to deploy Parse as a Kubernetes Deployment using the YAML as illustrated below:

```
apiVersion: extensions/v1beta1
kind: Deployment
metadata:
  name: parse-server
  namespace: default
spec:
  replicas: 1
  template:
    metadata:
      labels:
        run: parse-server
    spec:
      containers:
      - name: parse-server
        image: ${DOCKER_USER}/parse-server
        env:
        - name: DATABASE_URI
          value: "mongodb://mongo-0.mongo:27017,\
            mongo-1.mongo:27017,mongo-2.mongo\
            :27017/dev?replicaSet=rs0"
        - name: APP_ID
          value: my-app-id
        - name: MASTER_KEY
          value: my-master-key
```

Testing Parse

It is important to test the deployment and this can be done by exposing it as a

Kubernetes service as illustrated below:

```
apiVersion: v1
kind: Service
metadata:
  name: parse-server
  namespace: default
spec:
  ports:
  - port: 1337
    protocol: TCP
    targetPort: 1337
  selector:
    run: parse-server
```

After testing confirms its operation, the parse then knows to receive a request from any mobile application; however, you should always remember to secure the connection with HTTPS after deploying it.

How to Perform a Rolling Update

A rolling update refers to the process of updating an application regarding its configuration or just when it is new. Updates are important as they keep applications up and running; however, it is impossible to update all features of an application all at once since the application will likely experience a downtime. Performing a rolling update is therefore important as it allows you to catch errors during the process so that you can rollback before it affects all of your users.

Rolling updates can be achieved through the use of Kubernetes Replication Controllers and the kubectl rolling-update command; however, in the latest version, i.e., Kubernetes 1.2, the Deployment object API was released in beta. Deployments function at a more advanced level as compared to Controllers and therefore are the preferred mechanism of performing rolling updates. First, let's look at how to complete a rolling update with a replication controller then later using Deployment API.

Rolling Updates with a Replication Controller

You will need a new a new Replication Controller with the updated configuration. The rolling update process synchronizes the rise of the replica count for the new Replication Controller, while lowering the number of replicas for the previous Replication Controller. This process lasts until the desired number of pods are operating with the new configuration defined in the new Replication Controller. After the process is completed, the old replication is then deleted from the system. Below is an illustration of updating a deployed application to a newer version using Replication Controller:

```
apiVersion: v1
kind: ReplicationController
metadata:
  name: k8s-deployment-demo-controller-v2
spec:
  replicas: 4
  selector:
    app: k8s-deployment-demo
    version: v0.2
  template:
    metadata:
      labels:
        app: k8s-deployment-demo
        version: v0.2
    spec:
      containers:
        - name: k8s-deployment-demo
          image: ryane/k8s-deployment-demo:0.2
          imagePullPolicy: Always
          ports:
            - containerPort: 8081
              protocol: TCP
          env:
            - name: DEMO_ENV
              value: production
```

To perform an update, kubectl rolling-update is used to stipulate that we want to update the running k8s-deployment-demo-controller-v1 Replication controller to k8-deployment-demo-controller-v2as illustrated below:

```
$ kubectl rolling-update k8s-deployment-demo-controller-v1 --upda
```

Rolling updates with a Replication Controller faces some limitations, such that if you store your Kubernetes displays in source control, you may need to change at least two manifests to co-ordinate between releases. Additionally, the rolling update is more susceptible to network disruptions, coupled with the complexity of performing rollbacks, as it requires performing another rolling update back to another Replication Controller with an earlier configuration thereby lacking an audit trail. An easier method was developed to perform rolling updates with a deployment as discussed below:

Rolling Updates with a Deployment

Rolling updates with a deployment is quite simple, and similar rolling updates with Replication Control with a few differences are shown below:

```
apiVersion: extensions/v1beta1
kind: Deployment
metadata:
  name: k8s-deployment-demo-deployment
spec:
  replicas: 4
  selector:
    matchLabels:
      app: k8s-deployment-demo
  minReadySeconds: 10
  template:
    metadata:
      labels:
        app: k8s-deployment-demo
        version: v0.1
    spec:
      containers:
        - name: k8s-deployment-demo
          image: ryane/k8s-deployment-demo:0.1
          imagePullPolicy: Always
          ports:
            - containerPort: 8081
              protocol: TCP
          env:
            - name: DEMO_ENV
              value: staging
```

The differences are

- The selector uses match labels since the Deployment objects support set-based label requirements.

- The version label is excluded by the selector. The same deployment object supports

multiple   versions   of   the
application.

The kubectl create function is used to
run the deployment as illustrated below:

```
$ kubectl create -f demo-deployment-v1.yml --record
deployment "k8s-deployment-demo-deployment" created
```

This function saves the command
together with the resource located in the
Kubernetes API server. When using a
deployment, four pods run the
application to create the Deployment
objects as shown below:

As mentioned earlier on, one advantage
of using deployment is that the update
history is always stored in Kubernetes
and the kubectl rollout command can be

```
$ kubectl get pods
NAME                                                    READY      STATUS
k8s-deployment-demo-deployment-3774590724-2scro         1/1        Runnir
k8s-deployment-demo-deployment-3774590724-cdtsh         1/1        Runnir
k8s-deployment-demo-deployment-3774590724-dokm9         1/1        Runnir
k8s-deployment-demo-deployment-3774590724-m58pe         1/1        Runnir

$ kubectl get deployment
NAME                                  DESIRED    CURRENT    UP-TO-DATE
k8s-deployment-demo-deployment        4          4          4
```

used to view the update history illustrated below:

```
$ kubectl rollout history deployment k8s-deployment-demo-deploymer
deployments "k8s-deployment-demo-deployment":
REVISION         CHANGE-CAUSE
1                kubectl create -f demo-deployment-v1.yml --record
2                kubectl apply -f demo-deployment-v2.yml --record
◄                                III                                ►
```

In conclusion, rolling updates is an essential feature in Kubernetes, and its efficiency is improved with each released version. The new Deployment feature in Kubernetes 1.2 provides a well-designed mechanism of managing application deployment.

Statefulness: Deploying Replicated Stateful Applications

Statefulness is essential in the case of the following application needs:

- Stable, persistent storage.

- Stable, unique network

identifiers.

- Ordered, automated rolling updates.

- Ordered, graceful deletion and termination.

- Ordered, graceful deployment and scaling.

In the above set of conditions, synonymous refers to tenacity across pod (re)scheduling.

Statefulness can be used instead of using ReplicaSet to operate and provide a stable identity for each pod. StatefulSet resources are personalized to applications where instances of the application must be treated as non-fungible individuals, with each having a stable name and state. A StatefulSet ensures that those pods are rescheduled in such a way that they maintain their identity and state. Additionally, it allows one to easily and efficiently scale the number of pets up and down. Just like ReplicaSets, StatefulSet has an anticipated replica count field which determines the number of pets you want operating at a given time. StatefulSet created pods from pod templates specific to the parts of the StatefulSet; however, unlike pods developed by ReplicaSets, pods created by the StatefulSet are not identical to each other. Each pod has its own set of volumes, i.e., storage, which differentiates it from its peers. Pet pods have a foreseeable and stable identity as opposed to new pods which gets a completely random number.

Every pod created by StatefulSet is allocated a zero index, which is then utilized to acquire the pod's name and hostname and to ascribe stable storage to the pod; therefore, the names of the pods are predictable since each pod's name is retrieved from the StatefulSet's name and the original index of the instance. The pods are well organized rather than being given random names.

In some situations, unlike regular pods, Stateful pods require to be addressable by their hostname, but this is not the case with regular pods.

Attributed to this, StatefulSet needs you to develop a corresponding governing headless service that is used to offer the actual network distinctiveness to each pod. In this service, each pod, therefore, gets its unique DNS entry; thus, its aristocracies and perhaps other clients in the network can address the pod by its hostname.

Deploying a Replicated Stateful Application

To deploy an app through StatefulSet, you will first need to create two or more separate types of objects outlined below:

- The StatefulSet itself.

- The governing service required by the StatefulSet.

- PersistentVolume for storing the data files.

The StatefulSet is programmed to develop a PersistantVolumeClaim for

69

every pod instance which will then bind to a persistent volume; however, if your cluster does not support dynamic provisioning, you will need to manually create PersistentVolume using the requirements outlined above.

To create the PersistentVolume required to scale the StatefulSet to more than tree replicas, you will first need to develop an authentic GCE Persistent Disks like the one illustrated below:

```
$ gcloud compute disks create --size=1GiB --zone=europe-west1-b pv-a
$ gcloud compute disks create --size=1GiB --zone=europe-west1-b pv-b
$ gcloud compute disks create --size=1GiB --zone=europe-west1-b pv-c
```

The GCE Persistent Storage Disk is used as the fundamental storage mechanism in Google's Kubernetes Engine.

The next step in deploying a replicated Stateful application is to create a governing service which is essential to provide the Stateful pods with a network identity. The governing service should contain:

- Name of the Service.

- The StatefulSet's governing service which should be headless.

- Pods which should be allotted labels synonymous to the service, i.e., app=kubia label.

After completing this step, you can then create the StatefulSet manifest as listed below:

```
apiVersion: apps/v1beta1
kind: StatefulSet
metadata:
  name: kubia
spec:
  serviceName: kubia
  replicas: 2
  template:
    metadata:
      labels:                             1
        app: kubia                        1
    spec:
      containers:
      - name: kubia
        image: luksa/kubia-pet
        ports:
        - name: http
          containerPort: 8080
        volumeMounts:
        - name: data                      2
          mountPath: /var/data            2
  volumeClaimTemplates:
  - metadata:                             3
      name: data                          3
    spec:                                 3
      resources:                          3
        requests:                         3
          storage: 1Mi                    3
      accessModes:                        3
      - ReadWriteOnce                     3
```

Later on, create the StatefulSet and a list
of pods. The final product is that the
StatefulSet will be configured to develop
two replicas and will build a single pod.
The second pod is then created after the
first pod has started operating.

72

Understanding Kubernetes Internals

To understand Kubernetes internals, let's first discuss the two major divisions of the Kubernetes cluster:

- The Kubernetes Control Plane

- Nodes

- Add-on Components

The Kubernetes Control Panel

The control panel is responsible for overseeing the functions of the cluster. The components of the control panel include:

- The etcd distributed persistent storage

- The Controller Manager

- The Scheduler

- The API server

The components function is in unison to store and manage the state of the cluster.

Nodes

The nodes function to run the containers and have the following components:

- The Kubelet

- The Container Runtime (Docker, rkt, or others)

- The Kubernetes Service Proxy (kube-proxy)

Add-on Components

Apart from the nodes and control panel, other components are required for Kubernetes to operate effectively. This includes:

- An Ingress controller

- The Dashboard

- The Kubernetes DNS server

- Heapster

- The Container Network Interface network plugin

Functioning of the Components

All the components outlined above interdepend among each other to function effectively; however, some components can carry out some operations independently without the other components. The components only communicate with the API server and not to each other directly. The only component that communicates with the etcd is the API server. Rather than the other components communicating directly with the etcd, they amend the cluster state by interacting with the API server. The system components always initiate the integration between the API server and other components. However, when using the command kubectl to retrieve system logs, the API server does not connect to the Kubelet and you will need to use kubectlattachorkubectl port-forward to connect to an operating container.

The components of the worker nodes can be distributed across multiple servers, despite components placed on the worker nodes operating on the same node. Additionally, only a single instance of a Scheduler and Controller Manager can be active at a time in spite of multiple instances of etcd and the API server being active concurrently performing their tasks in parallel.

The Control Plane components, along with the kube-proxy, run by either being deployed on the system directly or as pods. The Kubelet operates other components, such as pods, in addition to being the only components which operate as a regular system component. The Kubelet is always deployed on the master, to operate the Control Plane components as pods.

Kubernetes using etcd

Kubernetes uses etcd which is a distributed, fast, and reliable key-value store to prevent the API servers from failing and restarting due to the operating pressure experienced by storing the other components. As previously mentioned, Kubernetes is the only system component which directly communicates to etcd, thereby has a few benefits which include enhancing the optimistic locking system coupled with validation, and providing the only storage location for storing cluster state and metadata.

Function Of The Api Server

In Kubernetes, the API server is the primary component used by another system component as well as clients such as kubectl. The API server offers a CRUD (Create, Read, Update, and Delete) interface, which is important for querying and modifying the cluster state over a RESTful API in addition to storing the state in etcd. The API server is also a validation of objects to prevent clients from storing improperly constructed objects. Additionally, it also performs optimistic locking, therefore, variations in an object are never superseded by other clients in the situation of concurrent updates.

It is important to note that the API server does not perform any other task away from what is discussed above. For instance, it does not create pods when you develop a ReplicaSet resource, nor does it overlook the endpoints of a service. Additionally, the API server is not responsible for directing controllers to perform their task; rather, it allows controllers and other system components to monitor changes to deployed resources.

kubectlis an example of an API server's client tool and is essential for supporting watching resources. For instance, when deploying a pod, you don't have to continuously poll the list of pods by repeatedly executing kubectl get pods.

Rather, you may use the watchflag to be notified of each development, modification, or deletion of a pod.

The Function of Kubelet

In summary, Kubelet is in charge of every operation on a worker node. Its main task is to register the node it is operating by creating a node resource in the API server. Also, it needs to constantly oversee the API server for pods that have been scheduled to the node, and the start of the pod's container. Additionally, it continuously monitors running containers and informs the API server of their resource consumption, status, and events.

The other functionality of Kubelet is to run the container liveness probes and restarting containers following the failure of probes, in addition to terminating containers when their pod is deleted from the API server and notifies the server that the pod has been terminated.

Securing the Kubernetes API Server

Think of this situation; you have an operational Kubernetes cluster which is functioning on a non-secure port accessible to anyone in the organization. This is extremely dangerous as data in the API server is exceptionally susceptible to breaches; therefore, you have to secure the API server to maintain data integrity. To secure the API server, you must first retrieve the server and client certificates by using a token to stipulate a service account, and then you configure the API server to find a secure port and update the Kubernetes master and node configurations. Here is a detailed explanation:

Transport Security

The API server usually presents a self-signed certificate on the user's machine in this format: $USER/. kube/config. The API server's certificate is usually contained in the root certificate which, when specified, can be used in the place of the system default root certificate. The root certificate is automatically placed in $USER/. kube/config upon creating a cluster using kube-up.sh

Authentication

The authentication step is next after a TLS is confirmed. In this step, the cluster creation script or cluster admin configure the API server to operate one or more Authenticator Modules made up of key components, including Client Certificate, Password, Bootstrap Tokens, Plain Tokens and JWT Tokens. Several authentication modules can be stated after trial and error until the perfect match succeeds. However, if the request cannot be authenticated, it is automatically rejected with HTTP status code 401. In the case of authentication, the user is provided with a specific username which can be used in subsequent steps. Authenticators vary widely with others providing usernames for group members, while others decline them altogether. Kubernetes uses usernames for access control decisions and in request logging.

Authorization

The next step is the authorization of an authenticated request from a specified user. The request should include the username of a requester, the requested action, and the object to be initiated by request. The request is only authorized by an available policy affirming that the user has been granted the approval to accomplish the requested action.

With Kubernetes authorization, the user is mandated to use common REST attributes to interact with existing organization-wide or cloud-provider-wide access control systems. Kubernetes is compatible with various multiple authorization modules such as ABAC mode, RBAC Mode, and Webhook mode.

Admission Control

This is a software module that functions to reject or modify user requests. These modules can access the object's contents which are being created or updated. They function on objects being created, deleted, updated or connected. It is possible to configure various admission controllers to each other through an order. Contrary to Authentication and Authorization Modules, the Admission Control Module can reject a request leading to the termination of the entire request. However, once a request has been accepted by all the admission controllers' modules, then it is validated via the conforming API object, and then written to the object store.

Securing Cluster Nodes and Networks

In addition to securing a Kubernetes API server, it is also extremely important to secure cluster nodes and networks as it is the first line of defense to limit and control users who can access the cluster and the actions they are allowed to perform. Securing cluster nodes and networks involves various dimensions which are listed below and are later discussed in detail:

- Controlling access to the Kubernetes API

- Controlling access to the Kubelet

- Controlling the capabilities of a workload or user at runtime

- Protecting cluster components from compromise

Controlling Access to the Kubernetes API

The central functionality of Kubernetes

lies with the API, therefore, should be the first component to be secured. Access to the Kubernetes API can be achieved through: Using Transport Level Security (TLS) for all API traffic - It a requirement by Kubernetes that all API communication should be encrypted by default with TLS, and the majority of the installation mechanism should allow the required certificates to be developed and distributed to the cluster component.

API Authentication - The user should choose the most appropriate mechanism of authentication, such that the accessed pattern used should match those used in the cluster node. Additionally, all clients must be authenticated, including those who are part of the infrastructure like nodes, proxies, the scheduler and volume plugins.

API Authorization - Authorization happens after authentication, and every request should pass an authorization check. Broad and straightforward roles may be appropriate for smaller clusters and may be necessary to separate teams into separate namespaces when more users interact with the cluster.

Controlling access to the Kubelet

Believe it or not, Kubelets allow unauthenticated access to the API server as it exposes HTTPS endpoints, thereby providing a strong control over the node and containers. However, production clusters, when used effectively, enable Kubelet to authorize and authenticate requests thus securing cluster nodes and networks

Controlling the capabilities of a workload or user at runtime

Controlling the capabilities of a workload can secure cluster nodes by ensuring high-level authorization in Kubernetes. This can be done through:

- Limiting resource usage on a cluster

- Controlling which privileges containers run with

- Restricting network access

- Restricting cloud metadata API access

- Controlling which nodes Pods may access

Protecting cluster components from compromise

By protecting cluster components from compromise, you can secure cluster nodes and networks by:

- Restricting access to etcd

- Enable audit logging

- Restricting access to alpha and beta features

- Reviewing third-party integrations before enabling them

- Encrypting secrets at rest

- Receiving security alert updates and reporting vulnerabilities

Managing Pods Computational Resources

When creating pods, it is important to consider how much CPU and computer memory a pod is likely to consume, and the maximum amount it is required to consume. This ensures that a pod is only allocated the required resources by the Kubernetes cluster, in addition to determining how they will be scheduled across the cluster. When developing pods, it is possible to indicate how much CPU and memory each container requires. After the specifications have been indicated, the scheduler then decides on how to allocate each pod to a node.

Each container of a pod can specify the required resources as shown below:

- `spec.containers[].resources.limits.cpu`

- `spec.containers[].resources.limits.memory`

- `spec.containers[].resources.requests.cpu`

- `spec.containers[].resources.requests.memory`

While computational resources requests and limits can only be specified to individual containers, it is essential to indicate pod resource and request as well. A pod resource limit stipulates the amount of resource required for each container in the pod.

When a pod is created, the Kubernetes scheduler picks a node in which the pod will operate on. Each node has a maximum limit for each of the resource type, i.e., the memory and CPU. The scheduler is tasked to ensure that the amount of each requested resource of the scheduled containers should always be less than the capacity of the node. The scheduler is highly effective that it declines to place a pod on a node if the actual CPU or memory usage is extremely low and that the capacity check has failed. This is important to guard against a shortage in the resource on a node incase of an increase in resource usage later, for instance, during a period peak in the service request rate.

Running OF PODS with Resource limits

When a container of a pod is started by Kubelet, it passes the CPU and memory limits to the container runtime as a confirmatory test. In this test, if a container surpasses the set memory limit, it might be terminated. However, if it is restartable, the Kubelet will restart it, together with any form of runtime failure. In the case that a container exceeds its memory specifications, the pod will likely be evicted every time the node's available memory is exhausted. A container is not allowed to outdo its CPU limit for extended periods of time, although it will not be terminated for excessive CPU usage.

Automatic scaling of pods and cluster nodes

Pods and cluster nodes can be manually scaled, mostly in the case of expected load spikes in advance, or when the load changes gradually over a longer period, requiring manual intervention to manage a sudden, unpredictable increase in traffic or service request. Manual scaling is not efficient and it is ideal, therefore, that Kubernetes provides an automatic mechanism to monitor pods and automatically scale them up in situations of increased CPU usage attributed to an increase in traffic.

The process of autoscaling pods and cluster nodes is divided into three main steps:

- Acquiring metrics off all the pods that are managed by the scaled resource object.

- Calculating the number of pods required to maintain the metrics at the specified target value.

- Update the replicas field of the scaled resource.

The process commences with the horizontal pod autoscaler controller, obtaining the metrics of all the pods by querying Heapster through REST calls. The Heapster should be running in the cluster for autoscaling to function once the Autoscaler obtains the metrics for the pod belonging to the system component in a question of being scaled. The Autoscaler then uses the obtained metrics to determine the number that will lower the average value of the metric across all the replicas as close as possible. This is done by adding the metric values obtained from all the pods and dividing the value by the target value set on the HorizontalPodAutoscaler resource and then rounding the value to the next larger value. The final step of autoscaling is updating the anticipated replica count field on the scaled component and then allowing the

Replica-Set controller to spin up additional pods or delete the ones in excess altogether.

Extending Kubernetes Advanced Scheduling

Kubernetes has an attribute of being an advanced scheduler; therefore, it provides a variety of options to users to stipulate conditions for allocating pods to particular nodes that meet a certain condition, rather than basing it on available resources of the node. Kubernetes advanced scheduling is achieved through the master API which is a component that provides offers to read/write access to the cluster's desired and current state. The scheduler uses the master API to retrieve existing information, carry out some calculations and then update the API with new information relating to the desired state.

Kubernetes utilizes controller patterns to uphold and update the cluster state where the scheduler controller is particularly responsible for pod-scheduling decisions. The scheduler constantly monitors the Kubernetes API to find unscheduled pods and decides on which node the pods will be placed on. The decision to create a new pod by the scheduler is achieved after three stages:

- Node filtering

- Node priority calculation

- Actual scheduling operation

In the first stage, the scheduler identifies a node which is compatible with the running workload. A compatible node is identified by passing all nodes via a set of filters and eliminating those which are not compatible with the required configurations. The following filters are used:

- Volume filters

- Resource filters

- Affinity selectors

In addition to scheduling, cluster users and administrators can update the cluster state by viewing it via the Kubernetes dashboard which enables them to access the API.

Best Practices for Developing Apps

After going through much of the content in developing applications with Kubernetes, here are some of the tips for creating, deploying and running applications on Kubernetes.

Building Containers

- Keep base images small - It is an important practice to start building containers from the smallest viable image and then advancing with bigger packages as you continue with the development. Smaller base images have some advantages including it builds faster, it has less storage, it is less likely to attack surface and occupies less storage.

- Don't trust just any base image -

Most people would just take a created image from DockerHub, and this is dangerous. For instance, you may be using a wrong version of the code, or the image could have a bug in it, or, even worse, it could be a malware. Always ensure that you use your base image.

Container Internals

- Always use a non-root user inside the container - A non-root user is important in the situation that someone hacks into your container and you haven't changed the user from a root. In this situation, the hacker can access the host via a simple container escape but, on changing the user to non-root, the hacker will need numerous hack attempts to gain root access.

- Ensure one process per container - It is possible to run more than one process in a container; however, it is advised to run only a single process since Kubernetes manages containers based on their health.

Deployments

- Use plenty of descriptive labels when deploying - Labels are arbitrary key-value pairs, therefore, are very powerful deployment tools.

- Use sidecars for Proxies, watchers, etc. - A group of processes may be needed to communicate with one another, but they should not run on a single container.

How to Deploy Applications That Have Pods with Persistent Dependencies

You can have applications having persistent pod dependencies using the Blue-Green Deployment mechanism. This mechanism involves operating two versions of an application concurrently, and moving production traffic between the old and new version. The Blue-Green deployment mechanism switches between two different versions of an application which support N-1 compatibility. The old and new versions of the application are used to distinguish between the two apps.

How to Handle Back-Up and Recovery of Persistent Storage In The Context Of Kubernetes

Persistent storage in Kubernetes can be handled with etcd which is a consistent and an essential key-value store since it acts as a storage location for all Kubernetes' cluster data. They ensure the correct functioning of etcd, and the following requirements are needed:

- Check out for resource starvation

- Run etcd as a cluster of odd members

- Ensure that the etcd leader timely relays heartbeats to followers to keep the followers stable

To ensure a smooth back-up, you may operate etcd with limited resources. Persistent storage problems can be eliminated by periodically backing up the cluster data which is essential in recovering the clusters in the case of losing master nodes. The Kubernetes states any critical information, i.e., secrets are contained in the snapshot file which can be encrypted to prevent unauthorized entry. Backing up Kubernetes clusters into the etcd cluster can be accomplished in two major ways: built-in snapshot and volume snapshot.

etcd clusters can be restored from snapshots which are taken and obtained from an etcd process of the major and minor version. etcd also supports the restoration of clusters with different patch versions. A restore operation is usually employed to recover the data of a failed cluster.

In the case of failure in the majority of etcd members, the etcd cluster is considered failed and therefore

Kubernetes cannot make any changes to its current state. In this case, the user can recover the etcd cluster and potentially reconfigure the Kubernetes API server to fix the issue.

How to Deploy An Application With Geographic Redundancy In Mind

Geo-Redundant applications can be deployed using Kubernetes via a linked pair of SDN-C. This is still a new concept developed in ONAP Beijing and involves using one site as an active site and the other site acting as a warm standby, which could also be used as an active site. The operator is tasked to monitor the health of the active site by establishing failures and initiating a scripted failover. They are also responsible for updating the DNS server so that the clients would direct their messaging towards the now-active site. A PROM component, which was added later on, can automatically update the DNS server and monitor health, thereby eliminating the need of having an operator. PROM relays the status of the site health and can make informed decisions.

4. Conclusion

In conclusion, while this guide offers you a good understanding of the essential components of Kubernetes, you have to carry out practical examples to gain a deeper understanding of the concepts. This guide only explains the basic functionalities, but does delve deeper into fundamental concepts. It is important to note that Kubernetes is a sophisticated resource for creating and deploying; therefore, you need to start with the basics as you go deeper into key functionalities. We hope this guide has been key in understanding the basic concepts of Kubernetes which are still a developing concept. Thank you

** How did you like the book? Could you spare some time and review it.

My Other Books available across the platforms in e-book, paperback and audible versions:

1. **Blockchain Technology : Introduction to Blockchain Technology and its impact on Business Ecosystem**

2. DevOps Handbook: Introduction to DevOps and its Impact on Business Ecosystem

DEVOPS
HANDBOOK

Introduction to DevOps and its
impact on Business Ecosystem

CODE PLAN BUILD TEST RELEASE DEPLOY OPERATE MONITOR

STEPHEN FLEMING

103

3. Blockchain Technology and DevOps : Introduction and Impact on Business Ecosystem

4. Love Yourself: 21 day plan for learning "Self-Love" to cultivate self-worth ,self-belief, self-confidence & happiness

LOVE YOURSELF

21 day plan for learning "Self Love"
to cultivate self-worth, self-belief,
self-confidence & happiness

STEPHEN FLEMING

5. Intermittent Fasting: 7 effective techniques of Intermittent Fasting

7 EFFECTIVE TECHNIQUES OF
INTERMITTENT FASTING
Stay Healthy,Lose Weight,
Slow Down Aging Process & Live Longer!

STEPHEN FLEMING

6. Love Yourself and intermittent Fasting(Mind and Body Bundle Book)

You can check all my Books on my **Amazon's Author Page**

** If you prefer audible versions of these books, I have few free coupons, mail me at valueadd2life@gmail.com. If available, I would mail you the same.

www.ingramcontent.com/pod-product-compliance
Lightning Source LLC
Chambersburg PA
CBHW071258050326
40690CB00011B/2441